Before First Light

Poems by John Binder

Dedication:

With deepest love and humility
this work is dedicated to dear Jeanne,
to Josh, to John Henry and Sharon.

f-stop
books

Published by F-Stop Books 2016

Copyright © 2016 John Binder

All Right Reserved.

ISBN-10: 0-692-74452-5
ISBN-13: 978-0-692-74452-9

Designed by Cindy Vance
Cover photo by Jeanne Field

This is a love song
to all the people
I've forgotten in my life:

I'm sorry,
I still love you.

Contents

Love Test — *1*

Before Dawn's Early Light — *2*

A Panther In Love — *3*

Montauk 1969 — *4*

If I Were A Dog — *7*

Cartoon Romance — *8*

Dreams and Other Fictions — *10*

Not Ever — *11*

Festival On The Moon — *12*

A History Of (My) Religion — *14*

Religious Education — *16*

Rocketry — *17*

A Found Object — *19*

Cut To: — *21*

I Found The Answer — *22*

Dear One — *23*

Don't Apologize — *24*

The Party's Over — *25*

Dead Aim — *26*

Finished — *27*

Fair is Fair — *28*

Keep On Riding — *29*

N.Y.C. — *31*

Upper Broadway — *32*

A Blind Eye — *33*

Compassion — *34*

A Documentary Poem — *35*

Billy 'n Apple — *36*

May 19, 1969 — *37*

Stories: — *38*

Faces — *40*

Kid McCoy — *41*

City Of War — *44*

Truth In Deception — *46*

Good Dead Reds — *49*

Don't Give Peace A Chance — *50*

Warriors — *52*

Cosmic Expansion — *53*

Rising — *54*

Mescaline Is The Exact
    Opposite Of Mayonnaise — *55*

Our Stoneybrook Farm — *57*

My Bay Mare — *58*

The Usual Apprehension — *59*

Bucky Among School Children — *61*

Poor Guy — *62*

The Big Letting Go — *64*

Truth — *68*

Despair — *69*

An End To Terror — *70*

Francois The Frog — *71*

In The Garden Of
    Emma Jamaica Rose — *73*

Eat More Possum — *74*

She Warned Him — *77*

A Fine Day For Education — *81*

Hieronymus Bosch Ranch — *82*

Care Less Love — *83*

Each Love Unique — *84*

An Orgy of One — *85*

Addicted — *86*

Hope — *88*

Existential Leap — *89*

Keep Looking — *91*

Extermination Blues — *92*

Hard Times Come To America — *94*

Hello, Dopey — *95*

Rub A Dub — *96*

Heart On The Line — *97*

I Think Of You — *98*

Look Not Back — *99*

July — *100*

Karma — *101*

Kennebunkport Cowboy — *102*

Leaves Of Grass — *104*

Leaving L.A — *105*

Losses — *107*

Love Curse — *108*

Love Is A Drug — *109*

Mainstream News — *110*

End Of Days — *112*

Leftovers — *113*

Morbid Thoughts — *114*

Time Bends — *116*

I Pet My Dog — *117*

Nature — *118*

No Theories - No Conclusions — *119*

Now — *120*

Old Flames — *121*

Our Grateful Dead March — *122*

P.O.V. — *124*

Paris, May 1968 — *125*

Pascal's Hesitant Pensées — *127*

Peace — *128*

Pirates Of The Pentagon — *129*

War No More — *130*

Cost Of War — *131*

Razor's Edge — *133*

Real Morning — *134*

Refraction — *135*

Premonition — *136*

Upheaval — *137*

Rock Bottom — *139*

Sally And Lee — *140*

Saved By Mutilation — *142*

Second Thoughts — *143*

See Ya — *144*

Seek And You Might Find — *145*

Cooler Than Average — *146*

Guilty As Conceived — *148*

Simply Survive — *149*

Solstice — *150*

Struck Down — *151*

Take Me In — *153*

Testing The Waters — *154*

Soaring — *157*

The End Is Nigh, ho ho hee — *158*

Empire Uber Alles — *161*

The Fourth of July — *163*

Killers — *164*

The Night Before Christmas — *165*

Rules Of Golf — *169*

Self Denial — *170*

The Shortest Distance — *171*

Grown Ups — *172*

Theology Of War — *173*

This Holy Holiday Season — *174*

Today's Forecast — *175*

Tremors — *176*

Try Harder — *177*

Wounds of War — *179*

Conscience — *180*

Under Your Thumb — *181*

You Don't Know You — *182*

Love Is Not — *185*

Unimaginable Magic — *185*

We Fight — *186*

Finished — *187*

I Think I'll Go Now — *188*

Goddess Of Love — *189*

Love Test

Looking deep into her heart, I asked:
Do you believe in poetry?

Believe in poetry?
What does that mean?

Simple sentences, or twisted ones,
chopped up, repainted, moved around
until they say something new?

Oh, I like poetry, yes.
But does poetry like you?

Stop it.
It stops.

I don't like clever people, she said.
You'll love me then, said I.

And she did...eventually.

Poetry made me do it, she confessed

Before Dawn's Early Light

We are bodies
we are strings
we are thin
shafts of weed
we are blades
of green grass.

In the dark
we are dew-covered
and some
country wind
moves us.

It will be
morning
fatally soon,
but now
everywhere
there are crickets
and tree frogs
and we are still
growing wildly
in their sound.

A Panther In Love

Good friends are hard
to come by.

You are no exception.

I've been lying
in wait for you
for a very long time.

I dare you to
walk under this tree.

Montauk 1969

A white wing-shaped kite
lies up on the wind
were it eddies
above the bluff.
We mistake it for a gull
and marvel at its stillness
but it can't adjust
to the updrafts
subtly as the birds do
and it has to be
tugged from below
giving away its lifelessness.

Nothing inanimate is good enough
for this matchless coastal day.

Dull mostly green marble-size
fox grapes bank the path
down to the beach.
Blackberries ripen
with curious selectivity
only half a dozen
purple ones to a bush.

My son sees his first snake
and his first toad,
minor discoveries
that thrill him on this day
two weeks after we watched
men walk on the moon.

The surf is powerful
beyond comment.

(No one has ever
said anything worthy
of man's reaction
to the sea)

There are surfers
scattered up the shore
like flotsam.
None ride for a moment
then one rises
wobbling at first
tentatively,
a practical student
of rudimentary physics
before the wave crests
and he kicks himself bravely
down the long wall.
Now he's marvelous
as the gulls
on the wind
over the bluff,
a boy on a board
riding waves.

My summer landlord
was saying how the towns
are trying to keep
these rough kids out
with their long hair
and their wildness
untamed.

God! It's landlords
and upstanding citizens
who should be excluded
from wild places
like this receding margin
of rare land,
unless they've got
some skill to share
phenomenal as riding waves
or sleeping on the wind.

If I Were A Dog

If I were a dog
you would love me,
a cute little pup
you would hug me.

You would feed me treats
and tickle my belly,
I'd lick your face
you'd laugh yourself silly
and you would love me.

We would walk in the park
like we used to.
You'd tease me 'til I bark
like I used to.
We would wrestle and play
all night and all day,

If I were dog
you would love me.

That little rascal
that you rescued
from the pound,
who romps all around,
you took away his gloom
He thinks you hung the moon

He loves you
he loves you
he loves you
almost as much as I do.

If I were a dog
you would love me too.

Cartoon Romance

She came bustin' in the door
raging and sputtering mad,
Yosemite Sam stormin' the saloon.
"Where's my damn heart", she said.
"You took it and tore it apart,
stomped it and threw it away."

"I never would have touched it,
or given it a second glance", said I,
"but you hung it out like a mail bag
to be hooked by some passing train.
A lotta girls are easy but you were
as eager as that cwazy wabbit."

Her eyes bulged out at that,
she rolled up her sleeves,
balled up her fists and flexed
her muscles like Popeye.
It was clear that she intended
to make mincemeat outta me.

It stopped her when I popped her
with a wet smooch on her kisser.
I know how to turn these bullies around.
Her eyes swam, her head swooned,
her knees buckled, she was going down,
but the bell saved her, ending the round.

But love's no simple boxing match.
Tighten your belt and tie your shoes,
it's a fight to the finish win or lose.
First you charm 'em, then you
disarm 'em with funny feelings
they've never ever felt before.

Oh, they've got their moves,
They'll juke and they'll jive.
They'll strip and they'll flip,
They'll run and you'll give chase
like the coyote after the roadrunner
right over that big cliff called love.
It won't break your bones, but
it sure can break your heart.

Looney Toons and Merry Melodies
playing wildly in your head,
cartoons leave you in stitches.
Ours ended in pain and tears instead.
that's all folks, all she wrote,
sad as when Bambi's mother died.

Dreams And Other Fictions

Last night, you know,
when you fell asleep,
I watched you hard
for a very long time.
Something had happened
in our bed to remove
any trace of the past,
any hint of the future.
I tried to remember you
as you were an hour ago.
I could not imagine
who you really want to be.

In the still and quiet
without memory,
without dreams
and other fictions,
your perfection
overwhelmed me.

Not Ever

Scrambled eggs?
Oh, wow!
Take,
she said,
that shit
from my sight.
Can't stand
proper food,
sufficient sleep
or short hair
on men,
not my precious men.

Eek!
Cleveland,
you haunt me
long distance.

She naked,
haunted,
sat,
skinny
in a cloud
of doubt,
exclaiming,
speeding again
hoping
to fly.

Festival On The Moon

OK in the pagan lights
scorching some girl's face
I smiled out of the crowd
because she was so inside out
and looking good that way,
her red soul flashing
from the hell of the Bronx.

Everyone around us on the hill
in the music and the deep grass
is smoking breathing swimming
like blind fish eating
each other one way or another.

Getting worse watching speed
freaks at work playing burning
themselves up in the hellfire
amphetamine.

Will they ever become
the Indians we dreamed?
Not Red Cloud
not Crazy Horse
not Brilliant Sequoia
not certainly not
the Sainted Joseph
the war chief
who gave up war forever.

Ghost dancers
on the moon perhaps,
this suicidal generation.

When's the resurrection?
Will the Beatles be there
reunited?
How much are tickets
to a wet dream?

A History Of (My) Religion

I once was friends with Jesus.
We talked frequently,
I felt his presence everywhere.
It was a beautiful feeling
which made me as happy
as any kid could be.

Then along came feelings
of a different kind.
Just an urge at first
they said it was a sin
to encourage it in any way
but alas I sometimes did.

I went to confession and
the priest asked me
if I touched myself
under the covers at night.
When I confessed I did
he insisted I describe it.

His interest was intense
and strange, I thought,
but I complied.
I asked God's forgiveness
but I was too embarrassed
to tell Jesus much about it.

Soon there were girls
in their warm and silken glory.
They made temptation worse
and I eagerly gave in.
"The spirit is willing,

but the flesh is weak"
they say that Jesus said.

No disrespect to Jesus
but experience soon told me
that willing spirit
and weak flesh together make
the strongest thing on earth.

If sex is a sin, I thought,
what in hell can holy be?
Sex is what came between
Jesus Christ and me.

Religious Education

At St. Mary
we got
a religious
education.
The nuns
used to
come down
the aisles
knocking
our heads
like practice
golf balls
or the tops
off dried
dandelions.

We prayed
like hell
for recess.

Rocketry

I was raised
on superstition
so the technology
of love
initially
confused me.

Bodies
seemed
exquisite
but dangerous
and complex
as modern rockets
beneath their
protective
shrouds.

For a while
I concentrated
on faces
which were
more rudimentary,
studying them
kissing them
but staying
safely away
from the intricate
hardware
down below
until I felt
competent
to try
my hand
at rocketry.

Later
would come
the moon, mars,
and fiery breakups
amid the brilliant
stars.

A Found Object

In her bed new mysteries
are found.

I am treasured here
in her plush home
among other things
she has chosen,
picked with a shrewd eye.
I am one of the objects,
favored more than the rest
touched often, caressed.

The other things
are just casually used
as she needs them,
whereas I am
in great demand,
a masterpiece
that she has found.

There is some light
in her room
and she appraises me,
gloating like a pirate
left unguarded
in the exchequer.

But she is deceived.

I am the outlaw here.
I have robbed the rich
before and will again.

With her finest gold
and silver in my pack
by the first light
I'll steal away.

CUT TO:

Int. Hotel Bedroom - Late Afternoon.
Love Scene.

We hide guilty and warm
in the light and dark
moving in slow motion
to prolong the ecstasy.

Crossfade

Now it is night.
Low sounds outside.

Your head on the pillow.
Your highly polished eyes
above everything.

Everything is better
than I expected

but then
I never expected you.

Fade to black

I Found The Answer

Walking with you on filthy streets
Riding with you in subways
even smashed up against
people who smell bad,
I'm wild!
I feel like screaming
"Alright, everybody get naked
and start singing!
Let's ride through the Bronx
this way!"

We walked down canal street,
hopeless canal street
amid the plumbing fixtures
and the used filing cabinets,
past the sheet metal works.
At the red light we danced
without even thinking about it
and the truck drivers stopped
worrying about immigrants
taking away their jobs
to blow their horns and
smile at me with envy.

After breakfast with you
listening to my theories,
I feel like a great demagogue.
I want to call a town meeting
and convince everyone
that America does
             have a future!

Dear One

The way you lean on
everything I say...

I didn't want to be
the one to tell you
there isn't anything
that anyone can do
for anyone
except to be there
part of the time.

Don't Apologize

We should know by now
it's impossible to be faithful
to dreams or to people.

The same desires
which keep us trying
defeat us invariably.

Monday
We fall in love.
It gives us wings.

Tuesday
one of us
will fly away.

The Party's Over

Please
turn out the lights.
Turn out our lights.

Put out the cat
that won't leave us alone
with our lives.

How can I possibly sleep
with so many tears for us
slogging around inside me
while I'm trying
to stay young and trim
for the apocalypse?

I'm not your lover anymore.
I'm just a country boy
wanting clouds.

I'm not your lover anymore,
but I desperately
want some for you.

Dead Aim

The phone at 4:00 o'clock
comes to your ear
like a high-caliber slug.

I'm the gunman
threatening you
long-distance.

You tell me
I'm calling too late.
You're already dead.

Finished

How can such simple things
end so painfully?
Friendships that turn to real disaster.
Friends wanting only what they need
become monsters.
Afternoons that begin brightly
end in total dark.
Whole lives and fragments of lives
bracketed with tears.

I don't want to touch anything now
that has people in it.
Not a bed for making love
or one for dying.
Don't want to hear a song where
someone is mentioned fondly.

I want none of it! All bets are off!
I'll take less animate objects
like stones, trees, the countryside,
highways, ants, rainstorms...
things that end without crying out
or calling attention to themselves.

Fair is Fair

I've been with some good women
I've been with some bad
I didn't deserve the good ones
The bad ones didn't deserve me

Keep On Riding

Funny thing.
Some people I've liked most
I've never gotten close to.
There are three or four others.
I think they are still alive.

God, boy, what happened
to your wonderful head?
It used to be
a mess of good things,
cracked thoughts,
shards of sunlight.
Now there's automobile glass
sticking in your eyes...oh...

No one knew you
no one knew you
and I won't tell stories
if you can't sing them.
Even I didn't know more
than three or four facts:
You never changed that sweater.
You hung out with real angels.
I don't know if you even owned
a pair of socks.
And like the papers said,
you crashed at four o'clock.

Someone from the college called me
the morning after your accident.
I was still at home in Pennsylvania
having not yet decided to return
to our zany monastery in Gambier.

Leahy dead? Christ!
You were just killed
like ordinary people get killed
on the highway late at night?
Nothing special? Just smashed
against a stone pillar, cracked open,
torn with glass and automobile tin?
Ordinary blood ran out and you died?
Fuck, Leahy!
Right there on a two lane road?
No tricks? No stunts? No magic?
Not even a little hip fake,
and some diversionary laughter?

Man, we used to drive that stupid road
flat out with you on the hood
of my little white sports car, laughing
and singing your drunken ass off
into the wind!

Passing farmers in their dirty trucks
knew we were nuts, but couldn't know
we had a deal:
We said only assholes got killed!

For a long time I figured
you were pulling a fast one.
I didn't go to your funeral.
I was like the Mexicans
after they got Zapata...

I knew you were still
on your white horse,
up in the hills.

N.Y.C.

Where I come from

we ate things like
Spam
and tomato sandwiches
a lot.

This city is crazy!
Who ever heard
of an egg cream
or a
fucking potato knish?

God,
I miss Pennsylvania.
I haven't heard
a screen door slam
a crow call
or an apple drop
all summer.

1969

Upper Broadway

Who can describe Upper Broadway?
Not me.
Dante couldn't.

Everybody up here
is missing something,
arms, legs, eyes...
friends.

People hang out windows
looking at things
no one wants to see.

1969

A Blind Eye

It was funky
down on Third Avenue
where Sharon and I
used to live.

The bums pissed
            slept
            and died
in the hallway
but I carefully
stepped over
everything.

Aren't we all
like that?

Compassion

On the bus tonight
across from me was
a woman with ugly legs,
scarred, veiny, fat,
like two huge squash
badly damaged in transit.
They were legs to win
a prize in a contest
for unpleasant features.

How would she take it
if she read this thing
and knew it was about her
legs that she lives with?

A Documentary Poem

entitled:

One Human Being Asking Another
For Directions From Hoboken To New
York.

        "Take da fuckin' tube."

Billy 'n Apple

Billy was a mean cat
but he had a soft spot
for Apple, who was a girl.
Billy used to drink and smoke
and hang around the block
kickin' ass and being nasty,
but when Apple came along
he would kid her and tell her
she was indeed the Apple
of his motherfuckin' eye.

May 19, 1969

Somewhat accidentally saw
a young Puerto Rican girl
get laid by a sailor in
Riverside Park down under
blooming lilac bushes near
the Westside Highway today.

Her hair was very long,
skin the color of tree bark.

Shouldn't have stayed but
couldn't leave unless
I wanted to disturb them.
So, I just watched quietly.

Didn't even feel guilty.
No sense in looking away.
Find it hard to describe
without unsightly metaphors.

My eyes are obsessed anyway.
Been very lonely lately.
Makes joy irresistible.

Stories:

The Second avenue bus
always carries loonies.
One very crazy guy
had a pillow on a leash.
He dragged it to the back
talking to it convincingly,
telling it to behave,
to sit and not to bark.
Everyone was laughing
turning around to look,
when the old man got mad
and kicked the pillow
the length of the bus.

Coming home one night
when we lived downtown,
I walked past this place
and someone hissed at me.
I looked up and
above me on the second floor
there was this naked guy
leaning out the window
grinning and jerking off.
I didn't wait to see
if a guy gets off like that.

Once on Fourteenth street
a man without any pants
staggered out of a whore house
with wounds all over his chest.
It looked like somebody
had squashed strawberries
on his white shirt.

He walked around showing us
that he had been stabbed
and asking what he should do.
Then a skinny black woman
came out of the building
wielding a butcher knife
and tried to put some holes
in the poor man's back.
It all happened strangely,
as if it were in slow motion.
I stepped between them
and kept her at bay with my foot.
The woman kept trying,
but without any fury, as if
she was just acting from habit.

When I first came to the city
from the sticks
and was afraid of everything,
a Puerto Rican lady
at the mouth of a dark street
asked me to carry her sleeping child.
"He's sick", she said.
"I'm tired and I don't know
if I can make it home.
It's four more blocks."
I'm still ashamed to admit,
I put my head down
and mumbled something
about it being late.
I didn't help her.
In those days I thought
Puerto Ricans were out
to get everybody and this
was some kind of trick.

1965

Faces

face of God
face of man
why distinguish
face of a child
face of the woman
who bore him
face of a flower
face of a daughter
equally adore them
brown face
white face
shades in between
why distinguish
all one human face
one human race

Kid McCoy

Kid McCoy is not a Panther
in spite of his black skin
and his also black beret.
Kid McCoy proclaimed sternly
in a saturated voice
that he was not drunk either.

Everyone else in the diner
prayed into their coffee
that this unnerving example
of real human suffering go away
and not interrupt their dinner.

He leaned on the counter, peering
at the man wiping it with a rag.
"Do I look drunk? Do I?"
The counterman wouldn't say,
he just turned and walked away.
"I'm just out of money...
out of money and starving.
Look at me. I'm hungry, man."

People got rigid, trying hard
not to look at a starving man.
"Gimme something you throw out.
You ought'a be able to do that."
He turned and looked down slowly
like a tragic actor finishing
a very poignant monologue.

There was silence for a long moment
as the diners struggled to subdue
their consciences and reclassify
the performer as a drunk, not a man.

"I'm not a Panther", he said,
politely sitting down with me,
and gesturing to his black beret.
"Don't worry, I'm not a Panther",
as if there were Black Panthers
looming in every white man's mind.
"I'm...well, you wouldn't know",
he said. "I'm Kid McCoy...er...
I used to be. They stopped me.
They wouldn't let me fight. Shit."
He looked down. "It don't matter.
My boy's dead. Got killed.
They put a bullet in his brain."

The thought ripped holes
in his mind and he looked away.
I tried hard to respond, but I was
locked in a fight with my conscience
about this poem I knew I'd gotten
when I bought him his meal.
"You didn't have to do this, man.
You didn't have to help me.
You're as black as I am, brother."
The compliment embarrassed me,
though I still cherish it today.

I studied his hands for relief.
They looked strong and oddly steady.
His eyes were a strong man's eyes,
shiny brown and slow moving.
His face was not badly marked
for the face of a fighter.
He felt the weight of my appraisal,
and his own sad circumstance.

With a sharp inhale of breath,
that startled me, he broke down
and started to cry.

My weak white merchant-class spine
was snapped straight by his tears.
I wanted him to be sober, young
and strong enough to join
the Black Panthers, and take back
his real name from whatever heartless
Irishman had dubbed him Kid McCoy.

I wanted him to be dangerous again.

1970

City Of War

In the city there is a broader
possibility of sorrow and confusion
than anywhere else.

Pain is more complex here,
being imported
from so many places
in its original
and purist states,
as the best distillates
are reserved
for the finest restaurants.

You can get wounds here
that just aren't available
in the provinces.

Some days the air
is filled with shrapnel.
New York is a monument to
and the capital of
the state of war.

For that reason,
and for many reasons,
it is a difficult place
to leave in one piece.

So many of us came here,
as fresh and raw recruits,
from the minor
cities and towns,
to join this proud old regiment,

which is being beaten badly
in a new and confusing war.

It doesn't seem right
deserting for the pleasures
of home, when so many others
must stay here, face down
in the future.

Eventually, given leave
by failure or success,
having lost face or nerve
we'll return to the country
to the suburbs or small towns
for more quiet wars.

We'll leave the City
to the poor and the dead.

Truth In Deception

Whispering in the bedroom
"Why can't we_____."
   Fill in the blanks for hours
   until daylight threatens
   as an unpleasant surprise.

I want guarantees against
meaninglessness and disappointment,
a little freedom in other words,
in case any promises I make
or have made turn out to be wrong.

Sound selfish?
A great virtue selfishness -
faith, hope and selfishness -
the greatest of which is
selfishness.
I've seen
what sacrifice does to people.
It makes them murderous.

She doesn't cherish freedom,
so she's willing to abandon it,
like giving up spinach for lent.

Turn on the light, PLEASE.
Do you need BOTH pillows?
Can't we get some sleep?
No, I NEED to talk this through.

Cigarettes and explanations.

Do I really want her?
Apparently, she still wants me.

I am continuity
in her speculation
about the way it can be
if you make the right
investment.

Of all the people in my life
I've attracted by reciting dreams
she's the one who believed me.
Now, she's shocked that I'm agnostic.
How could she imagine I might be
opposed to dreams coming true?
    Possible Epitaph:
    He found Satisfaction
    Perished immediately
I wonder about the theories
I've espoused, and the experiments
I've done to test them.
    My testing is done exclusively
    on humans, which is unethical.
    Generally, I don't mention it.

Adultery is despicable,
but like any art or science
it takes dedication.

Truth is a description
of how things worked
when the world was a pendant
hanging on a golden chain.
We had no need of orbital theory.
It was all straight lines
and simple measures.

Science is a way of working, merely.

Now that I am threatened here,
I wonder what conclusions
I'll concoct to get me
where I'm going.

By four o'clock she's satisfied
I don't do anything to hurt her.
She's bought my reasonable story.
She doesn't know I haven't got
the courage to intend hurting,
or to stop it when it seems
to be getting me my way.

I hate myself for everything.
I wish that she could take
just a little of the blame.

Good Dead Reds

I learned
on the news
tonight
we killed
37 communists
in Viet Nam.

All of
our guys
who got it
today
were capitalists,
except one.

They said
before dying
he renounced
any interest
in economics.

1969

Don't Give Peace A Chance
(With apologies to J. Lennon)

Don't give peace a chance,

Don't ever
give peace
the slightest chance.

Club it.
Smother it.
Kick it in the ass.

All I am saying
is don't
give peace a chance.

Knock it to the ground.
Step on it's throat.
Hold it down.
Beat it.
Stab it
'til it
bleeds to death.

Peace is bad for Business.
Peace don't sell no rockets.
Peace don't sell no guns.
Peace don't fly no
Aero-planes.

Peace is no damn fun.
Gimme a gun.
Don't be a fairy.
Be a mercenary.

Get over your depression
Become a Hessian.

Be tough.
It's the only virtue
we got left.
No faith.
No hope.
No charity.

Love and Kindness?
No siree.
Jesus Christ
Couldn't sell that stuff.
Just be tough.

Peace is for pussies.
Don't be a fairy.
Be a mercenary.
Get over your depression
Become a Hessian.

Don't listen to
that old song.
Johnny Lennon
had it wrong.

Everybody sing.
Everybody dance.

All we are saying is
don't
give
peace
a fucking
chance!

Warriors

Our killers are heroes
Theirs are martyrs
But warriors' brains
are all washed the same
Ours are professionals
Theirs are insane
Their bombs blow up
crowded market places
Our bombs rain down
on people's houses
Who will take
all these madmen from us
or beg them
to join the human race?

10/22/08

Cosmic Expansion

No one knows for sure
what really happened.

People, once indifferent,
suddenly touched each other
and caused an explosion
so that things changed
in the terrible heat.

It is said, everyone
became what he always
wanted to be...and
there was even enough
to eat.

Rising

The girl on my bed
curved over her guitar
picking notes
like berries
on a summer hill.

In the white room
the sunlight softened
even her light voice
and bleached the morning air.

It's a nice way to wake a man,
better than alarming him
with kisses, to wake him
by pouring music in his eyes.

Mescaline Is The Exact
Opposite Of Mayonnaise

Here I am again
on my back
at the start
of another new life.

My son is visiting me.
He and some kids he met
are sleeping over tonight,
all modern children
with run-away daddies
who do their drugs
guiltlessly
and have new mommies
in the dark.

Quiet, quiet, quiet...

Then they all start
coughing from their
sleeping places.
The coughs are crisp
and come at random
like the sounds you hear
around a country pond
or it could be
a garden of children
growing in the dark.

Good God! This painful life
is full of gorgeous sensations.

The drug is working.

The lights outside
multiply astronomically.
Someone nice is touching me,
a breeze of fingers
streaming all around.

Tonight doesn't even
smell like the city.

Quiet, quiet, quiet...

Then the children
are coughing
in their beds again,
crisply and at random.

Like I said,
it could be
a garden of children
growing in the dark
or the subtle serenade
from a country pond.

Our Stoneybrook Farm

It's mostly under asphalt now.
You wouldn't notice it behind
the gas station, the trailer lot,
the drive-in and the new motel
but the old farm we had
was a lovely place
with a big square brick house,
bluegrass pastures and
a sliver of stream thick with
silver minnows and watercress.

I remember my mother packed
tomato sandwiches for lunch
the first day we went
to watch the men begin
remodeling the old house.

I was very young and
I learned to ride there.
It was the place I was taught
so many of the pleasures
and all the cruelties
I would ever need to know,
how things are born,
perfectly grow and then
are made to die.

Ah, well. Such memories live
at least as long as we need them.

My Bay Mare

I had a bay horse once
who was nearly perfect.
She was young and fast
with fine legs and a head
that might have been
sculpted in the Renaissance.

One night, heartbroken
and nearly out of grace,
I raced her to the river,
ten cruel miles
on a white sand road
in the August dark.

Along the way
I became ecstatic.
I heard music in the fields
and sensed a voice that said,
"love isn't always available, son,
that's what beauty is for."

The Usual Apprehension

Something wakes me...
a passenger jet
                lowering itself
over the city

ready to flop on La Guardia
like a fat drunk falling
                on his girlfriend
in the dark.

                Outside
there are kids laughing
and talking in the street.

Nice sounds...
                kid's voices
at night

full of lovely idleness
                and bravery.

It's a pleasant night
                for New York
this time of year
not so full of
                the usual apprehension.

                I stay awake
smoke and entertain myself

                with thoughts
of a brilliant future.

                Now
it's quiet.

Suddenly, sirens up Broadway.

A fire?

Is there war on 125th street?

Bucky Among School Children

I once heard Buckminster Fuller
explain the universe
in an afternoon
to a bunch
of school children in Palo Alto.

It was wonderful.

As the old man
left the classroom
the kids cheered him
like a famous athlete.
They hadn't learned
to be demure
with great men.

I fully expected
some twelve year old
to brightly announce
that Mr. Galileo
will speak tomorrow
at 2 o'clock
in the cafeteria.

Poor Guy

I met a man
with grey skin
in a bar
in a town
in Oregon.
His hand shook
when he tried
to find his mouth
with a cigarette.

He was pitiful
and friendly
so I rode
to Vancouver
with him
in his old car.

We talked
about life.
His sounded
like a very
carefully described
train wreck.

Across the flats
of the Oregon desert
where driving
took no decision
he looked calm
in the splintered
light of the dashboard.
He was strong enough
to be bitter.

But in a little town
near the state line
the choice of roads
confused him.

I took the map
and tried
not to watch
when he cried.

We found Vancouver
by accident,
but he'd forgotten
the name
of the friend
he was driving
up to see.

While we waited
for his mind
to work
he told me
how his wife
had taken up
with his friend
while he was
in the hospital.

He wept again
when he got
to the part
about her
also taking
the house trailer.

The Big Letting Go

Elegy for Dale Eunson

You died like an eagle,
though you chose
to live like a dove.
It was the bravest thing
I've ever seen.

You were so majestic
as you looked
"it"
in the eye
and took the measure of
it for us.

"In spite of its terrors,
it is nothing,"
you told each one of us.

"The void is nothing," you said,
"even though you scream at night
in your dreams,
when you are falling into it,
down an elevator shaft,
into nothingness itself,
it is nothing,
so there is nothing to resist."
You smiled, audaciously.

In the horror dreams
you said you clawed
at the slick steel sides
of it's bleak nothingness
as you fell,

and you could not get a foot
or a finger-hold on anything.

This dream occurred over and over,
you said.
It was horrifying,
worse than anything you'd ever
experienced lucidly,
or on drugs,
or in fever dreams

until you stopped clawing
and digging in your heels
and just... fucking...
went with it!

"Falling takes no effort," you said,
"if you do just go with it.
And then it's not falling,
it's soaring, in fact."

Dear Dale,
entire religions are built upon
the hope of reaching
that big "letting go."

Each one has a name for it,
grace, nirvana, enlightenment,
but names diminish
the thing itself
as names so often do.

You summoned up all your panache,
like that stingy-brim hipster hat
you are wearing in the snapshot
on our refrigerator.

Now you've got a broken neck
from some hideous cancer
that sent it's roots
into your spine
like a tree cracking concrete.

A stiff plastic collar
and your eagle spirit
hold your head up straight.
Your back hurts.
The pain in your liver
is excruciating.

"But it's nothing.
Nothing is nothing, after all,
and I am not afraid of it," you said.
"A minute is like a year to me now.
I want to spend the time
I've got left enjoying the people I love,
and who love me,
not just cringing and holding on."

Katherine Hepburn, in character,
with all her panache
could not have said it better.
That's who I think
you wanted to approximate.

In your stories,
you describe your parents vividly:
your father, a foreign correspondent,
your mother, a WW2 woman
equal to any man.
You so admired
how they had strolled
through the fields of death

describing the fires of hell
back in their violent time.

You vowed to live that way yourself,
courage under fire,
so you reported on the void to us
as your father had reported the war.

We'll see you later, Dale,
every one of us.
Time will impose no restrictions then,
so let's make it Paris in 1946.

We'll all wear trench coats,
and rakish hats,
and smoke cigarettes,
drink wine and fall in love
with other dashing international misfits.

Adieu, Dale,
until we meet again.

(February, 2005)

Truth

The truth
shall make you...
scared.

Despair

Here I am
a defeated man.
I bit off more
than I could chew,
a tasty morsel
of broken glass
so gut-slashed
I can't hold water
let alone dreams.
I am exhausted
and will suspend
this futile search
for a single
incandescent soul
to warm myself by
and accept that
human harmony
is just a body
in the dark,
just a spark,
not a wildfire
nor a heaven
filled with stars.

An End To Terror

There does come a time
when the usual terrors
we have lived with
just don't work anymore.

This may be the only gift
that maturity brings
besides a cold heart
so that love can't
hurt you again.

I have looked forward
to this fierce calm
I hoped would come
when I wouldn't have
to get drunk
to punch reality
in the nose.

Ah, the usual terrors
just don't work anymore.
How intoxicating!

Francois The Frog

Francois the Frog
doesn't like water.
He won't go near it.
He just can't bear it.
He keeps his little green carcass
firmly on the land.

Frank loves the beach.
He adores the sun.
He likes to sit in the sand
and sip the occasional pina colada.
He just does not like
that darn cold wet water.

Frank is from France,
born in a tank,
real name Francois.
That's French for Frank.

You know what they do
With frogs in France.
They catch 'em.
They cook 'em.
They eat 'em, you see,
and Frank had no intention
of ending his very sweet life
in some frickin' fricassee,

so Frank crossed the ocean
on a very slow freighter.
He met a lovely amphibian
and started to date her

but when they got to the states
she ran off with an alligator.

Damn shameless amphibian,
he wished she'd stayed in France
and somebody would've ate her.

In The Garden Of Emma
Jamaica Rose

To: Emma Jamaica Rose Styron-Larson
on her very first birthday

In the Garden of
Emma Jamaica Rose
the snakes wear sneakers
with bells on their toes.

They eat marshmallows,
kumquats and dates.
The fireflies travel
on roller skates.

There's mommy and dad
in the bifocal tree
with heartburn and earmuffs
watching tropical fish
smoke their coco puffs.

The only law there is levity
since they rescinded
the law of gravity.

Nobody ever frowns
and everything flows
in the Garden of
Emma Jamaica Rose.

1989

Eat More Possum

So, I was headed for L.A.
driving across endless Texas
in a bad-ass V-8 Chevrolet,
that my ol' man had given me
after a couple accidents
he couldn't quite remember,
and they wouldn't let him
drive it anymore.

The weather had been rough.
A wicked ice storm, they call
"a Blue Norther" down there,
had it's deathly arms around me
the whole damn way.

Cars were going off the road.
A big eighteen wheeler truck
got turned over by the wind,
right in front of me.
I stopped to check the driver.
He was OK. Another trucker stopped,
so I drove away and kept
charging hard through the storm.
Along about Dallas, it eased up.

I drove on to Austin
to visit an old friend, Kit,
his cute little girlfriend, Pup,
and his unusual brother, Goat.
Only in Texas do they name you
after a stupid smelly animal
and you wear it proudly
the rest of your life.

We drank a bit, smoked a lot,
told stories and did whatever
it was we used to do back then.
Nothing eventful happened,
'least nothing I want to admit.

When the storm was gone
the Chevy and I moved on,
headed for my future in L.A.

Way out in the country,
about a mile from nowhere,
I stopped to buy gas
and a sixpack of beer,
which was my traveling
companion in those days.
It was just a crossroads store,
with one gas pump outside,
and two old tobacco-spitting
codgers sitting on the porch.
I had long hair, back then,
which was the fashion,
Except in rural Texas
and such places god forgot.
Long hair was girly to them.
You had to always be ready
for ridicule and worse,
if it came to that.

I put the gas nozzle
in the filler-up pipe,
nodded to the geezers
on the porch, who nodded back
and spit in skillful unison.

I washed the windshield,
topped off the gas tank,
put the nozzle back, and
went inside to buy my beer.

Now, Kit, or Goat, more likely,
had put a bumper sticker
on my car, a joke, a play
on the advertising slogan,
"Eat more beef".

That slogan and another,
"Goat ropers have more fun",
were popular in Texas then.

My new bumper sticker said
"Eat more possum." Ha, ha.

I couldn't get the sticker off,
so I'd left it on the car.

When I came out of the store,
with a six-pack in my hand,
one of the old rednecks was up
and squinting at my bumper sticker.

I didn't know what to expect,
but I expected something ugly.
The squinty old man in overalls
looked past me toward his buddy
and said, country dry, "Hey, Harv,
look at that. This young fella,
cain't even spell pussy."

The moral of this story is:
don't judge a man
by the way he spits tobacco.

She Warned Him

There were many more than one
"Lone Star" over Texas
and the scene I came upon
in the predawn light.

The sun was not up yet.
There was no color at all.
It was like a charcoal sketch,
from the old frontier.

I stopped my car to take it in.

Cowhands seemed to be asleep
in their saddles, cigarettes dangling
from their lips as their ponies
moved carefully, side to side
in a slow dance-like motion
not to disturb the dozing riders
or the doomed steers that
they were carefully holding
in a huddle near the fence.

All were waiting for the trucks
to come and load the cattle
to take them to their execution.

I said a prayer for the animals
and the people we city slickers
depend on for our sustenance.

Just a few miles down the road,
as the sun was busting the horizon,
I stopped at a roadside diner.

Eggs, bacon, pancakes and coffee,
"The All-American Breakfast",
was billed on the menu, proudly,
with two little American flags.

Maybe I'd get a trumpet blast,
and my patriotic breakfast served
by a Dallas Cowboy Cheerleader,
though it's not very likely
anybody would dare to startle
a roomful of redneck Texans
waking slowly over their coffee
at that hour of the day.

The counter waitress, Linda Ann,
her name above one breast,
was no Dallas Cheerleader.
She silently squinted at me.

A beefy trucker in a feed store hat,
claimed the stool next to me.
He looked all around and asked,

"Where's Betty this morning,
Linda Ann? She sleepin' in?"

"She's over to the hospital."

"Hospital?! She alright?"

"She's alright, but he ain't."

Linda Ann didn't say who "he" was.
The trucker apparently knew.

"What happened?"

"She shot him."

The trucker grunted softly,
as she described the scene.

"He come over there, drunk.
She told him to go away.
He said he'd kick the door in.
She said she had 'papers' and
she'd shoot him if he did."

They nodded mutually, as if
words were in short supply.

"He kicked the door in."

"And she shot him?"

Linda Ann slid the coffee-creamer
toward him, and leveled her gaze.

"She warned him."

The trucker reset his cap,
the only emotional gesture he had.

"Is he gonna live?"

"Maybe. She's over there waiting."

Linda Ann turned away
to attend to another customer.

The trucker lit a cigarette,
sipped his coffee and farted.

I quit breathing for a moment
and leaned over my food.
I tried to imagine the woman
who shoots her man and then

stands vigil at the hospital
to see if he is going to survive.

I managed to eat only about half
of my "All-American Breakfast".

Linda Ann met me at the register.

"I couldn't help but hear", I said.
"Don't mind if I ask what'll happen
to your friend Betty for shooting
that guy, especially if he dies?"

"Nothin' "

She looked at me with tolerance,
knowing I wasn't from around there.
"She warned him."

What more to say?

The sun shined bright,
when I went outside
convinced I'd gotten a glimpse
deep into the heart of Texas.

A Fine Day For Education

In the morning my friend Bill,
organic farmer and philosopher -
sometimes the other way around -
sat in the kitchen thinking aloud.

  "We all suffer from indirection,
  or maybe call it misdirection.
  I live next to a dairy farm.
  They send the milk to the city
  sixty miles to be pasteurized,
  and packaged, then they ship it
  back here to the local store
  where I go and buy it.
  From now on I'll just walk over
  to the farm next door for my milk."

Later in the day I was talking
to an old man who said simply,
  "When anyone, any place, anything
  hurts me, I don't go back no more."

In the evening, I read "Black Elk Speaks".
In one of his visions he heard a voice,
  "Behold a good nation, walking
  in a sacred manner, in a good land."

At night I fell asleep thinking
very hard about America.
and what we must do to survive.

Hieronymus Bosch Ranch

The countryside seems ill tonight,
darkly foreboding as a horror movie.

The moon's a sickly street lamp
looming yellow over the valley.

A young owl imitates a grown-up owl,
unconvincingly, out by the barn.

The fresh-cut steers moan and drip
blood from holes where their horns
and their testicles used to be.

They are condemned to a feed lot
to be fattened for the butcher's knife.

The coon hunters are down in the ravine
with their whisky, guns, and dogs
barking after their terrified prey.

The people in the rickety old house,
lovers once, now torture each other
with grim and terrifying subtlety.

The valley is still and dry as tinder.
No fog lumbers in from the coast
to salve the murders of the day.
A random spark could set it all off.

Then God forbid.

Care Less Love

I gave over whole parts of my life
to people who used me badly,
much worse than I would have
if I hadn't given myself away.

I have tried long and hard to find
the weakness that allowed that atrocity.

My son, Josh, nailed it, one day,
when he turned to me and said,
"Dad, you and mom did Johnny and me
no favor when you raised us to be polite."

Is it that simple? If you're too nice,
they will wrest your soul away?

Each Love Unique

Singers forever sing
and poets crow about
the gorgeous girls
they've loved,
or the masterful men
who stirred their souls,
broke their hearts,
took them high,
laid them low.

That song never ends
and never gets old.

Each love unique
in its fashion
echoes in eternal passion.

An Orgy of One

Such wild delight.
You seem to be
seven women
under me tonight.
You change
like a gambler's luck.
Just close your eyes,
hold your laughter
and your tears
'til all of us are done.

Addicted

I think I'm addicted
to sobriety.
I'm really enjoying
this normalcy.

I gave up the bottle
and I gave up the pipe.
The three of us
had a terrible fight.

Now, I don't get high,
but I don't get so low.
Right down the middle
of the road I go.

There's a ditch on the right.
On the left there's a chasm.
You son of a bitch,
stay away from my wagon.

I never had thought,
that I would abstain
'til it quickened my heart
and slowed my brain.

The drink made me to shake.
The smoke made me shiver.
They made my head throb,
and my liver quiver.

I hated to quit
what I did best.
but when you wear it out
you gotta give it a rest.

For quite a while, now,
I've been sober.
Yippee tie yie yay,
I'm a damned teetotaler!

Hope

Something's trying to get born here
Something's trying to kill it

The house is on fire
The sky needs to rain

Everybody wants change
Nobody wants to change a thing

Go stop the sunrise
Shoot the wind with a bullet

Something's trying to get born here
Something's trying to kill it

Existential Leap

It sounds like magical thinking
but it's entirely provable fact,
when threatened with extinction
man and animal, tribe or pack,
to save the entire family
must make what scientists call
an "existential leap".

When dire necessity dictates
the brain expands, ideas come
which never were had before.
A starving chimp suddenly
will use a stick to probe
the honey from the tree.
Birds learn to communicate
across the expanse of the sea.

Human beings harnessed fire,
lighting grass with a spark,
used a hook to catch fish.
The marvel of electricity
allowed us to see in the dark.
We defied gravity by flying
to the moon and aim for Mars.

We have the means now
to save ourselves,
threatened as we are.
Machines and devices
have multiplied our strength,
expanded our brains.
They have given us genius
we have never had before

but our will has withered,
our persistence is gone.
The tribe' is in a panic.

We furiously fight on the deck
of this burning sinking ship.

The next leap we must make,
is in our heart, not our brain.
Love is man's only salvation.
Peace is our existential dream.

Our brains are already bursting
with ideas and invention.
Survival of all must become
our truly sacred intention.

Love is the magical thinking.
When will we embrace it?

Keep Looking

Know yourself,
Socrates told us
way back when,
but try as you might
all day and all night
with every device
the last person
likely to know who
you really are
is most likely you.

Ask any acquaintance,
old or new,
their first appraisal
will likely get closer
to what is true
about the real you
than ever will you.

It is hard to see
the person who lies
behind your own eyes,
but that, my dear,
for worse or better
is definitely you,
so, keep looking.

Extermination Blues

"Bye bye, love.
Goodbye happiness.
Hello loneliness.
I think I'm a gonna die."
                    The Everly Brothers

I used to enjoy life
when it was new,
in every way,
now, in only a few.

Little things mean a lot
but don't add up to much,
if little things
is all you've got.

Every day used to be
a new page
in a great book.
Now, I mostly watch TV.

Stocks are down.
Murder is up.
Whom shall we
bomb today?
I'm trying to
make sense
before is is was
and I am past-tense.

Adapt or die,
old Darwin said.
Change your heart,
or change your head.

Change your underwear
and your dirty socks
is what my darlin' wife
would have said.

Hard Times Come To America

Companies fold
Factories close
Jobs disappear
Thieves loot the banks
Con men sell worthless paper
Life savings vanish
The government
stands by and watches
then joins the looters
sending good money after bad.

We were living in fat city
now there's nothing
but teeth and bones
We must stick together
to survive this
Don't leave anybody out
We'll soon discover
What we're made of
And what we're really worth

We ought to hang the bastards
that did this
but what's the use?
It's hard to forgive them

Maybe we should skin 'em
and roast 'em
and eat 'em
like a Christmas goose.

12/28/08

Hello, Dopey

You look dopey
when you step off the plane
like your mother
made you wear your
rain boots to a dance.

You walk all funny
and your lips are canted
like you have a caraway seed
pinned in your front teeth.

I know you put your glasses
in your pocket so you'll look
pretty coming down the ramp
and indeed you do
but even when you squint
you don't see me standing there.

When I say your name
and put out my hand
you freeze like a rabbit
in the headlights of a truck.

And then you change,
and you look like a woman
who came three thousand miles
just to make a man smile.

Rub A Dub

You would make a great bathtub.

When I've spent all day in you,
I feel cleaner.

Hours later I sniff my skin
and there are traces of you
faint as talc.

Heart On The Line

Pass me the dice, Mr. Croupier,
I'm putting
my heart on the line.
I could win big
or lose it all this time.

I'm all in
I'm gonna let it ride
It's all been said
It's all been tried.
Deal me a card,
dealer man.

I'm all in
Let it ride

Love is a gamble
Love is a game
Lose your shirt
Or lose your name.

Truth
Fiction
Love
Addiction.

Give me them bones, baby.
Tonight we're rollin' high.

Let it all ride!

I Think Of You

You were once
       so elusive
made of light
       perhaps
a quick reflection
a random note.

I thought of you
as something fragile
       a crystal cup
       a brittle leaf
       a twig

love.

Now I think of you
as something heavy
       a storm
       a stone
       an office building.

I approach you
like a business appointment.

Look Not Back

Looking for love
is a bad habit
especially looking
where you left it.

Love lost
can't be found.
Leave the bodies
in the ground.

Immortal love
does exist.
Feel free to dream,
but don't insist.

It's accidental.
It's magic.
Lost love
is simply tragic.

July

Unbuttoning
buttons
Unlocking
doors
Sticking
our heads
out windows
to look
and to breathe
each other

Karma

The third law of motion states
that for every action there is
an equal and opposite reaction

I shove you
you move away
I pull you
you come back to me

That's physics

The law of Karma
is about the same

What I do to you
you will do to me
I hate you
you hate me
I love you
you love me too

The laws agree
You and I
can never be free

Take my hand
embrace me
we are connected
for eternity

Kennebunkport Cowboy
George W. Bush

They say he hails
from faraway Maine.
He rides the Texas range
in a bulletproof limousine
looking for someone to kill.

No one can touch him
with his posse all around,
men with little plugs
in their ears, who
whisper up their sleeves.

He lynched a hundred fifty men
back in the day,
and one battered woman,
whom he mocked
on her way to the grave.

Now, there's half a million
notches on the handle of his gun.
His fat little sidekick,
Dirty Dick, stalks old lawyers
and shoots 'em in the face.

The odds run against
the Kennebunkport Cowboy -
"Injuns" all around him -
still he'll squint and tell ya,
Custer didn't cut and run.

His heroes at the Alamo
stood tall with blazin' guns,
'til they were shot

full of holes by "Meskins"
and left to rot in the sun.

Down to his last few bullets,
there's one more fight to go.
He wants to meet Osama
one on one, high noon-style,
in the middle of the street.

Both are stone killers.
Both can shoot straight.
With a little luck
their aim will be true.

7/10/07

Leaves Of Grass

Leaves of grass
Shards of glass
Love me
or leave me
Kiss my lips
or kiss my ass

Leaving L.A.

To Susanna and Darrell on their departure
to a non-euphonious place.

I tried to tell to tell 'em
you can't leave L.A.
any more than you can walk out
on Bunuel's dinner party

but friends are strange creatures.
You take 'em to your heart.
You get to depend on 'em.
You realize you love the bastards
then they up an move to some place
called Nyack.

Nyack?!
Hard to write a poem about it.
Only thing it rhymes with is
- of course and god forbid -
kayak.

Darrell, I have known for ages.
Did a movie together when we first met.
Later we did a play together at the MET.

Only once or twice
we almost killed each other.
Isn't a friend that
you only want to kill sometimes
more like a brother?

I love Susanna.
Whenever there is a crowd around

she is often the only one
I want to talk to.

Susanna shoots from the hip
and seldom misses.
She has freckles and political conviction.
She looks good in summer dresses.

But to hell with friends
who move away to Nyack.
Move to a place that rhymes
with something beautiful,
a place that suits your own
exquisiteness like...

the Valley of the Blue Nile,
the Costa Brava,
the mountains of the moon.

Anyway I still say
you can't leave L.A.
any more than you can take the
intoxication
out of a bottle of
- oh my god it rhymes -
cognac.

Losses

If I could sing heartbreaking songs,
had memorized lyrics
of extravagant emotion,
knew speeches to say to you
that captured my dejection,
I would be beneath your window
wailing of my losses
until dawn drove me off
slumped in solitude and sorrow.

Unfortunately, I am unskilled,
ineloquent, and far too reserved
for such expressions of self-pity.
I am forced to say things straight,
to tell you I am sorry, I feel lousy
and I blame every last goddamn
big and little thing on you.

Love Curse

Everyone is bound to love you
as I did
and they will as I did
stop.

And you will forever wonder why.
Oh, dramatically "why?"
Oh, painfully "why?"
Oh, lovely "why?"
Oh, lonely "why, oh why?"

Oh! Om! No one home.
You will always wonder why.

Yesterday I said goodbye
to the parts of you
that hate me.

The parts of you that love me
I have captured
and I will keep.

And you will miss them
sorely
all the rest of your days.

And so will they
who try to love you
after me.

Ha! Ha! Hey!

Love Is A Drug

Love is a drug
Love is a trip
One little dose
can get you ripped.

But you don't need
pharmaceuticals
to be thrilled
down to your cuticles.

Drugs are unpredictable.
There's good ones
there's bad ones
sometimes all in one.

Bummers as low
as the ocean floor,
highs as high
as the bluest sky.

Our love
is a super drug,
a phantasmagorical
psychedelic trip!

Oh, good lord,
I am totally ripped.

Mainstream News

I'm not a real news person
I just play one on TV
The news that I deliver
does not really come for me

They're not my facts I'm reading
not my truths
nor my lies
my opinions
my conclusions
my exclusions
nor my surmise

Things come over the wire
someone captures them
someone writes them down
someone hands them to me

The little red light flashes
the director counts me down
I'm clueless
and empty as can be
I check my hair
I clear my throat
I read everything evenly

I don't just read
I act a little bit
If the news is grim
I frown
If it's funny
I chuckle or smile
If it seems dubious
I raise an eyebrow.

I'm not allowed
to be too forceful
or passionate
which makes me kind of glum.

Sometimes I feel like
storming the station
and taking myself hostage
with a gun.
Then I could report on it
like a real newshound

It would be a great story
Will the hostage live or die
Should they negotiate
or send the SWAT team in
after this desperate guy?

I'd cover all the action
with verve and alacrity
I'd consult with experts
in the law and psychiatry

I'd find the reasons why
someone with so much promise
would put a gun to my head
and cause so much distress

Maybe I'd bring it all
to a peaceful end
so the viewers can relax again
But a violent bloody climax
would make my ratings soar
and provide a fitting capper
to my TV career

7/15/07

End Of Days

At this dry
and narrow
end of life
excitement is gone
anticipation
luminous instinct
all gone
bleak vision
dull reason
and dread
remain

We still long
We still lust
We still hunger
We still crave
but we know
not to expect
satisfaction

Nothing left
but flickering life
and it is not the same
as living
brilliantly blind

Leftovers

Baby you bring out
the best in me
then you chase
it all away
and just the worst
is left of me.

Couldn't you leave
just a little bit
of something
worth saving
for somebody else
to chew on.

I came to you
full of
hope and dreams.
I left in tears
blood running out of
the holes you made.

I will survive
and I will find
someone
who brings out
the worst in me
and helps me
throw it away
until just
the best
is left of me.

Morbid Thoughts

At this stage of life
when I wake up at night
I think of death
and other things
I'd rather not.
Death comes peacefully
sometimes - sometimes
it's full of pain.

I watched my father die.
Mother's death I missed.
His came fast,
hers little by little.

My dad was tough,
an old school man,
noble to the end.
We had a final talk.
He asked softly,
"are you back
with your wife?"

I quickly wondered,
is it wrong to lie
to a dying man?
"We are talking
about it," I lied.
He softly said,
"They need you."

We had two boys.
He was right
and as my father
he was obliged

to stoke my guilt
to the end.
That's what fathers
are forever for.

I saw him cringe
as pain hit him.
I moved to the edge
of his bed
to caress him.

"No", he said,
"sit there".
He pointed to
a bedside chair.
I almost laughed,
it was so like him
not to accept pity.

I just watched
in silence then.
He was done with me.
Death was coming.

Soon he stiffened.
His eyes went wide.
His mouth opened
in a silent scream.
His breath rattled
and thus he died.

In the middle
of the night
I wonder how it
will come for me?

2016

Time Bends

When you get old
time bends back on itself
like a Mobius strip.
What was going to be
has now been.

Dreams are memories.
Gone is everything
in between.
Don't even ask
where did it go?
What did it mean?

Time bends,
we break
and disappear,
then return
as a memory.

I Pet My Dog

I pet my dog
and I feel like a child again.

My wife smiles
and I feel satisfied.

My son is mad at me
and it hurts like a bullet.

Who can explain
what love is?

I pet my dog
and I don't care.

Nature

Oh, what a beautiful day.
The large eat the small.
The quick sometimes
get away.

Choirs of birds
defend their homes
with vicious harmony.

As humans work to destroy
every vestige of humanity,
mother earth plots
our destruction,
catastrophically.

On such a gorgeous morning,
I glory
and I despair.

No Theories - No Conclusions

City in a very foul mood
Traffic clogging the streets
Raucous and confused crowds
smelling of terrible contempt
Old ladies cheating on line
Angry cabbies bursting veins
Salesmen arrogant as cops
More old ladies feeding birds
No motives just time energy
sole purpose end frustration
Air overhead is rancid icing
on this putrid urban cake
Dog shit and litter underfoot
Sounds even thicker than air
Walls sweat ragged ethnic music
Hope floats away with garbage
on the viscous Hudson River
Races case each other honkies
niggers P.R.'s chinks and jews
weighing chances in the coming wars
Everybody missing something
arms legs teeth eyes friends
More old ladies raving on Bway
Deaths unnoticed and unlisted
Kids screw on playground swings
No space no place to hide.
Everybody here from somewhere
didn't get what they came for
Break heads slit throats stomp
rape smash forget why exactly
Not one good fanatic even bothers
to run for public office
No theories, hence no Conclusions

Now

The day after yesterday
The day before tomorrow
No future
No history

The minute after
The minute before
The minute before
The minute after

This second is
The first second
The only second until
the next second arrives

Then is here
This is now
There is no other
Only this is

Enjoy it before
it is was
and is gone

Old Flames

I am getting tired
of these old flames
who never die out!

I meant to call you
at five o'clock
but then Larry came by
and we got very high.

You're fifty-caliber
phone call
brought me down.

Our Grateful Dead March

Sound off, one, two.
Sound off, three, four...

Sign them when they're very young.
Give them money and a gun.
Drill them 'til they're really numb.

(Sound off, one, two. etc.)

Drive them hard all night and day.
Another video game to play,
this one is far away.

(Sound off, etc.)

We can fight them over there,
or we can fight them over here.
Fight for all that we hold dear.

(Sound off, etc.)

Say it loud,
and say it proud,
smoking gun or mushroom cloud.

(Sound off, etc.)

Hell is hot,
the desert's hotter.
Kiss goodbye your son or daughter.

(Sound off, etc.)

Their brave deeds
are what we need
to satisfy our corporate greed.

(Sound off, etc.)

American boots on distant soil.
Every war has got it's spoils.
Trade their Blood for foreign oil.

(Sound off, etc.)

Play them music when they die.
Turn the volume up real high.
They won't hear their mothers cry.

(Sound off, etc.)

Bury them with medals later.
Put their pictures in the paper.
Claim they made our country safer.

ONE, TWO, THREE, FOUR
SOUND OFF!!

7/8/07

P.O.V.

I must be wrong
the way you see it,
but I know
what's right for me.

If I could turn
my inside out
you'd see me as I am,
and love me like
I want to be.

I don't care
about strangers anymore.
And I only have
a few good friends.
No one else matters.

So reach in here
and turn me
inside out
and see who
I want to be.

Paris, May 1968

In Paris
we went out
with our press cards
camera and recorder
to run with the students
and sample the excitement
of revolution.

But we were like
the boy in Faulkner's
story of "the Bear".
We wanted to be
simpatico
with the kids
in the street,
but our instruments
were too strong a link
to order and civilization.

They were no protection
against tear gas
and batons,
but they excluded us
from knowing
the wildness
that the crowd knew.

Whatever risks we took
playing daredevil
at the barricades
was insufficient.

Even my own blood
and yours

from injuries
the drunken riot cops
inflicted
were a way of lying,
flamboyantly.

I think the blood
just made me ashamed.

That happened before
when we'd gone to
record great sorrows
and historic events.

Sympathies matter,
but professional intentions
are always obscene.

A young person lies dead
in the street!

Click!

        Got it.

                Great pic!

Mortality abstracted.
The kid is still dead.

Pascal's Hesitant Pensées

I think
therefore
I think
maybe
I am
or maybe not.

Who knows?

Peace

Peace is not a dream
    nor mere aspiration
Peace is not a dream
    nor mere aspiration

Peace is love
    made manifest
Peace is love
    made manifest

Peace is life
    war is death
Peace is life
    war is death

Peace is our
    very breath
Peace is our
    very
        deepest
           breath

Pirates Of The Pentagon

We used to call them traitors
who obscenely profited from war.
Now they're shrewd businessmen,
not traitors any more.

They once were mercenaries,
who got paid to fight our fights.
They are "contractors" these days,
by their dim moral lights.

G.I. Joe and G.I. Jane
get paid a few dollars a day.
The Pirates of the Pentagon,
need trucks to haul the booty away.

Why fight for honor,
When you can fight for gold?
These modern warriors
are not the knights of old.

Sell them planes
and sell them missiles,
with a good hot war,
business sizzles.

"Money is not moral"
is the profiteers' line.
They pledge their allegiance,
to the bottom line.

While brave young patriots
die in the desert heat,
the traitors get rich on victory,
and just as rich on defeat.

7/12/07

War No More

"I will fight no more forever"
Nez Perce Chief Joseph said,
when his tribe had lost a war
against us a century ago.

Now as the world melts
and the lethal climate
threatens to kill us all,
why do we kill each other
in war after endless war?

All could be lost already
by our mindless belligerence.
What is the point of war,
if there is nothing left to win?

Even if we could kill
all the bad guys in the world,
who would the good guys be?

What would be left of our soul?

Cost Of War

What's it like to send them
over there?

How do you feel when
they come back home in a box?

Why were you for it,
before you were against it?

You knew damn well
it was wrong from the start.

Or were you just playing
both ends against the middle,

calculating?

Stop the calculation
of how many votes you'll get,
how many votes you'll lose.

Start the calculation
of how many lives you've taken?
All you men of war!
All you women of war!

What's the cost in souls and bodies?
That's the cost of your fucking war!

They lie
They lie to me
They lie to you
They lie
You die
They lie
cry cry

"It's Shock and Awe",
alright,
"my fellow Americans",
as LBJ used to say,
in another war
back in the day.

It's shocking and awful
the killing you do.

Did you ever look at it
from the other side?

Bullets coming through the walls
of your house.
Rockets coming through the roof.
Hide your babies under the bed.
Hold them tight
until they're dead.

Did you ever look at it
From the other side,

from their side,
from our side,
my twisted sisters and brothers
of America?

Razor's Edge

While the world sleeps
on a razor's edge,
I lie awake at night
and wonder which way
the blood will run.

It's a nightmare.

Someone tugs at my ankles.
Others yank my wrists.
They drag me back and forth
on the razor's edge.
Hope, despair.
Hope, despair.

It severs me in two.

Even as I perish
there is nothing I can do
but still passionately care.

Real Morning

Startled by daylight
morning comes to Manhattan
in the sacred faces
of the work force,
in their coughing
from first cigarettes,
in their slow moving
to old duties,
in their gestures
of habitual reluctance.

Real morning comes hours
before the successful folks
are roused by the gentle
tinkling of alarms,
by showers fresh and warm,
to bravely dare the subways
or perform their ritual breakfast
with the Times.

Real Morning is brutal
and muscular and honest.
It doesn't smile and cajole
and lie to hustle its wares.
It smacks you in the face.
Those who meet it squarely
are the best of the human race.

Refraction

She's always changing faces.
She's a million photocopies
of herself,
each one slightly altered
by the partly-silvered prism
of her dreams.

For now I am her dreams.

I am her dreams
and I can feel the sunlight
filter through my skin
refracting in my flesh
it comes out rainbows
in her eyes.

She is the sky.

She is August mornings
above the crystal river.
She is nights
when no one wants to sleep.

She is the light.

She is the softly changing
all infusing
elusive
morning light.

Premonition

What are you taking from me
when you lurk in the curve
of my body?

I don't know if...
there is anything I can give.
All my days have no conclusions
and then at night in our bed
something comes over me
and I am scared to death.

So, I talk to you
and try hard to disappear
inside your body.

Can you see how afraid I am
before we turn ourselves on
and for a while after
until we fall asleep?

Sometimes, even while
we are fucking
I can't help thinking
"If this doesn't work
what do we do?"

Upheaval

These past few weeks
our two lives have been moved
like twin peaks of some mountain,
heaved and cracked.

The fault under us is lifting, shifting
with thunder the great boulders
of things we have shared.

I think granite
immobile for centuries,
thousands of centuries,
would strain less and strained
would settle easier than we are
with this disturbance.

Is it possible
such bonds have grown
from interest seeded
so tentatively?
        I remember them formed
with fragile
        rays of light
          atoms of trust
mere touches
        wishes
        a wisp of saliva
between our lips.

Can we possibly survive
apart now -- severed,
fields between us
        space
determinedly traversed
together?

Or will we be like
the victims of some
famous operation --
and will they send
reporters daily
            to inquire
of our health for the news
and photograph us
roller skating in Brooklyn
or riding the ferry
alone
            but smiling
risking catastrophe
            every minute
we dare existing
            apart
with merely our frail
            separate organs
            to maintain us?

Perhaps we should stay
just a wind's distance
like trees in the same
            stand.

Rock Bottom

He was very alone.
He was at rock bottom.
He was at spiritual zero.
Even the devil wasn't there.

He sat on the his bed
with his hand on his cock
and felt the blood pumping
out of his soul.

He watched the sunlight
shriveling slowly
slither out the window
and disappear.

He closed his eyes
and tried hard
to make himself
go with it.

Sally and Lee

Sally, lovely soft sleek
nice sweet clever easy kind
curling curvy.
           Not ever mean.
Just 18.

Lee, pretty much the same
but with jagged edges.

         Mysterious
as the forest after dark.

She worked as a waitress
at a summer ice cream place
         called Blinkey's.

Used to serve me wild berry pie
a la mode and write love notes
         on the check.

It's how they caught her cheating:
"Coffee - 50 cents. (over)
I'm not wearing any panties
tonight! Can you tell?"

We sat under trees at the lake
drinking Genesee beer and
discussed suicide, three nights
before she disappeared.

I took refuge with Sally after that.
Sally cool lovely soft sleek nice neat
sweet...

But I wondered always about, Lee.
Did she do what we had discussed,
by the lake or did she just decide
to haunt me forever by her
ghostly disappearance?

Saved By Mutilation

I slog down Broadway Tuesday morning
and wonder about this persistent guilt
that has dogged me since childhood.

I wonder if I have forgotten
some important youthful dream
or broken some sacred promise I made.

The nuns used to try and scare us,
or maybe they meant to inspire,
by preaching about missionaries
who got their fingers chewed off
by some very pissed-off Indians
until they renounced their faith.

I don't know where they got that one,
but they delighted in scaring us with it.

It was hard not to be struck by that story
and for a long time I did expect my soul
might be similarly saved by mutilation.

Just now I passed a beggar on the street
who has no legs and yet I see no Indians
around this ferocious part of Broadway.

Second Thoughts

Second thoughts on the non-violent
revolution inspired by the patrons of an
Alabama ice cream stand as I approached
with a black woman to buy milk shakes.

I'd
like
to be
a man
but I'll
survive
if I can.

You lie
on the tracks
down here,
Mahatma,
and these
charming
country
cocksuckers
will change
your mind.

See Ya

I knew him way back...
when a dime was a dollar
now a dollar is a dime.

I knew her before
women got tattooed.

...back when
we had pay phones.

... back when
gas was cheap.

Now he's gone as cheap gas
and she and I
soon will be, too.

Seek And You Might Find

He's tried Religion
He's tried love
He's tried industry
He's tried art
He's tried politics

For a while he even tried getting by
without doing anything to help himself.
But even doing nothing didn't work.

So, one day he sat down and went mad.

Now they tell me he feels much better
though he lacks some of his earlier
ambition.

Cooler Than Average

My friend Ophelia was cool.
She jump off a building
leavin' me a note says
"I did it for the experience."

I didn't dig it right off, but
then I figured she was jes'
trying to face a cat she had
tol' me about some time back.

Dude was gonna be executed
by guys from a rival gang
in about a hour and a half
for somethin' he did that
they took offense at.

The bangers ask the cat
if he have a last request?
He think about it, then he say,
"I guess I wanna take a nap,
so I be fresh for the big event."

Dat so cool it blow Ophi's mind.
She need something she think
totally ape shit to top that.
I ask Ophi what 'cool' is, one time.
She say, "You gonna do somethin'
worth talkin' about for a while,
it better not make much sense."
I say, "Break dat down for me.
I don't follow dat too much."

"Dig what Jesus did", she say.
"He trick them Roman soldiers
into hanging him from a tree.
The guineas blame it on the Jews.
Now folks be hatin' all a them,
an' lovin' Jesus ever since."

"Now, that be cool", she said.

Guilty As Conceived

I was born feeling guilty
I'll die the same way.
Many things I'm sorry for,
I didn't even do.

Simply Survive

In order to survive
it is necessary
to simplify,
you told me repeatedly.

Complexity is suicide.

So, like everyone else,
I polarized my thoughts.

I divided neatly
what I love
from what I hate.

Now my heart
is an armed camp.

Not a feeling stirs
without the threat
of retaliation.

I am pitifully alive.

Solstice

Like all of you
I was young and brilliant once.
I'm old now and dumb as a dunce.
Now that my hair is white as snow
and some of my teeth are starting to go
I look back on autumn, summer and
spring
to savor the memories
this longest night of the year can bring.
Some of them cruel and some of them
kind,
they slip down the sinuous slopes
and the soul-jarring moguls
of my gradually crystallizing mind.
Say what you will about getting old
it terrifies the weak,
and mortifies the bold,
but it is packed with rewards
and the pleasures it hoards
can be savored like wine
as I sit by the fire
in the cold cold wintertime.

Struck Down

For My Mother Mary LaPorte

The hundreds of miles
I drove to be with you
after the shock
of the Captain telling me
what had happened
were nothing compared
to the light years
between my expectation
and my recognition of you
lying there as they had put you
on your side on the white bed
mangled and out of place
as airplane wreckage
in what they called "intensive care"
which means merely that someone
may be watching,
or will soon discover
when you have died.

I thought "God, what a bastard
you are (if you are)
to have dreamed up this
this horrid end to a beautiful life".
You laid there like that
for more than a year, immobile,
only your eyelids could move
and two fingers
but you were lucid, mostly
and you would cry when I
came to visit.

You would manage to laugh
when I said something funny.

Oh, how I loved you, mother.

Take Me In

When it's happening
and you get worried
because you feel it
starting to happen
you just have to run out
and start searching faces
like an old duffer looks
for his last golf ball
or a woman goes after
her lost best earring.

When it's happening
and you get that worried
you can go through faces,
I mean a lot of faces,
until it's almost got you
and then you get lucky
- maybe you get lucky -
and it's in someone's eyes
that they can take you
inside like a deep breath

And so it goes away
for a while.

Testing The Waters

He watched her for hours
until the lights of the store
blinked for closing time.
He must ask her now.

His reason for hesitation,
she was older than him,
closer to being a women,
than he to being a man.

Tonight was a deadline.
He'd thought about it all day.
She was alone
by the soda cooler.

No more waiting.
He approached her slowly
and asked carefully,
"can I walk you home?"

"What? I'm afraid
you might be afraid
of the dark or afraid
of me in the dark", she said.

Birds he had never heard
rushed from her throat
singing as she laughed
derisively.

Badly wounded,
he staggered
from her eyes
into the dark

trying to know
how he should feel.

There was nothing
in his ear now but
her terrible reply
and the felt sound
of his rapid pulse,
although the night
and the mountains
were loud around him.

He had rehearsed
so hard their walking
home together that
his loneliness was
a state of shock.

A broken bottle
left his brain and
menaced her face,
but he called it back.

He passed the lake
and had a flash
of himself drowning
and one of his friends
giving her
the tragic news.

He imagined her
scratching the sand
with her toes
and laughing again.

That thought freed him.

There are shooting stars
in the Summer sky.
You watch them and
you have to wonder
about the meaning
of everything.

Even with so little
experience, he knew
her cruelty had to be
exceptional.

By the time
he got home
he was wondering
who his next love
would be.

Soaring

The children soar
heaven-high
on bright balloons
of fantasy.

May time
let their dreams out slowly,
and bring them gently
back to earth.

The End Is Nigh, ho ho hee

Oh how we used to laugh
at those old cartoons
that showed a scrawny guy
with a beard and shaggy hair
carrying a sign that read,
"Prepare to meet your maker.
Repent, the end is near."

The backwards-yearning folks
in church, mosque and temple,
who dote upon the rants
that mad desert poets uttered
thousands of years ago,
took up the desperate chant,
"these are the end days.
repent, repent, repent.
It's (almost) all over now,
baby blue, Armageddon is just
around the corner from you."

All good sinners know
that crooked preachers preach
to fleece us of our money.
So we laughed and made fun.
and enjoyed our sinful ways,
until the weather changed.
Now fires rage, floods flow,
and these horrifying wars
come one upon another.

Is this the end of our world,
or just a period of change?

Mankind has adapted before.
This time we aren't so sure.

Now the crazy old man
in sackcloth and sandals
carrying that sign,
ain't so funny anymore.

*

The Traditional Hopi People,
whose time in this hemisphere
outdates the bible and Koran,
have a scripture they live by.
It's not written on paper,
but inscribed on their souls.
It's called the Hopi Prophesy.

Traditional Hopi, like Tibetans
and some other ancient tribes,
feel responsible for the lands
that sustain them, our land, too.

They feel it in deeper
and more mysterious ways
than we are able to.

Their most sacred spot of all
is the Black Mesa in New Mexico.
It is a mountain made of coal.
The ancient Hopi Prophesy
warns that if the Black Mesa
is destroyed, as we are now
devouring it to mine that coal,
our whole world will wither and die.

Now science and our common sense
tell us what this ancient prophesy
warned of all along, and the old man
with the beard and rags warned us, too.
As the world heats up and the ice melts
ancient truth and today's news agree.
The end indeed is nigh, ho ho hee.

Empire Uber Alles

As Empires fail
they flail
and speed their fall
by spending their wealth
on foreign wars while
starving those at home.

It would be
better called
committing suicide
by self-defense.

Look around you.
Any enemies you see?
We must go there
and everywhere,
hither and yon,
looking for targets
and villains to bomb.

Any fools out there
not in Congress yet?
Recruit them
Vote for stooges
to perform
rituals of idiocy.

We need soldiers
to be killed in war,
put in boxes
draped with flags,
and put medals on.

If we run out
We can get more
with stirring ads
on the Super Bowl.

The Fourth of July

Fact: On this day many years ago
Thomas Jefferson and John Adams died.

Today is the fourth of July.

Mourn for America, my friends.
Democracy is under attack.
The president would be king.
Benedict Arnold is next in line.
Oh, for revolution again,
Paul Revere to rouse the Patriots,
Tom Paine to steel our spine,
George Washington to lead us,
Sam Adams' furious mob
to tar and feather
the traitorous swine,
torch their greedy mansions,
ride them out of town on a rail.
Today is the fourth of July.
Celebrate America, my heroic friends.

Revive Democracy again.

7/4/07

Killers

The stone-hearted killers
with gleaming white teeth
fatty thick necks
and sharkskin suits
cruise the halls of Congress
smelling blood money
and some slick lobbyist
to buy them lunch.

10/22/08

The Night Before Christmas

'Twas the Night before Christmas and
Jesus was lonely.
Next morning would bring his birthday
He'd be thirty-three.
He was on the brink of a very bad year.
He could feel it coming, perhaps,
like a slow rolling storm,
or an evening fog up the valley.

He had that kind of intuitive mind.
But if he had forebodings,
he had no one to express them to.
His entourage, his disciples, the boys –
as he called them, collectively –
were gone for the holidays,
or the holy days of Hanukkah.
Mary was gone, Mary Magdalene,
gone off with his mother Mary,
somewhere.

It was funny how they got along,
the two Marys, a virgin and a whore.
He felt good about that.
It made things easier
that they were friends,
and it proved something, too.
Women have more open hearts than men.

Joseph was around but he was -
like most fathers of the old era -
unable to communicate.
Truth be told, there wasn't much
for them to talk about.

They had nothing in common
- Jesus, with his brain big as the universe,
and Joseph, a simple carpenter –
not even a bond of blood between them,
if legend is to be believed.

Of course, they loved each other
but it was an inarticulate affair.

Jesus thought about going to town
For a glass of wine,
but it was awkward when
he tried to socialize.
People tended to fall silent
around him, or pepper him
with questions about this and that.
They knew he was special.
Everyone could feel it.
Some held it against him.

"Who does he think he is?",
the Pharisees would mutter.
They said he was full of himself,
big for his britches or whatever
they called them in those days.

The open-hearted ones among them
just liked to bask in his attention.
Either way, Jesus didn't really feel
a part of the crowd, any crowd.

He went outside and sat on a stone
and looked at the stars in the sky.
Maybe he smoked a strong dark
Middle Eastern cigarette
and thought about things.

He pondered the state of the world.
It was in a sorry condition,
as it always was and always will be.
He wished he could do something
to wise people up and get them
to have consideration for each other.

He thought about the magic
He'd learned in Egypt when he was young,
when the wise men spirited him there
for an esoteric education.
But magic, no matter how enchanting,
is just tricks to attract a crowd,
like the Indians charming snakes
or the Africans and their trained monkeys.
Jesus knew that the real magic
was in the human heart.

That's what he tried to teach
the crowds that gathered round him.
Not just Moses' commandments,
about the way we should all behave,
but the magic of the heart,
which he knew - we all know - is love.

If you love completely, he preached,
you cannot sin.
The Commandments are unnecessary.

But the piece d'resistance of his teaching -
to coin a phrase in a language
which had not been coined yet –
was the thought with which he intended
to revolutionize the human race.

That concept was "forgiveness".
If you forgive unconditionally, he taught,
the sins of others will be diminished.
If you forgive yourself,
peace will rule the world.

Just reviewing these thoughts,
as he sat outside on the rock,
brought Jesus contentment.
He snubbed out the butt
of his cigarette, stood up,
took one last look at the sky,
whispered a prayer to his father
and accepted his fate that this
was the year he would die.

Rules Of Golf

(for Alex' 18th birthday)

Hit the ball
With the stick,
And try to keep it
Outta the crick.

If it slices or hooks,
Into the pond it goes.
Don't wade in the water
Up past yer nose.

On to the green
Into the cup
If it takes ten strokes,
Who gives a fuck.

Hit the ball
down the middle
If you need to win
just cheat a little.

Self-Denial

I knew a girl
who loved me,
who said
she could not
have me,
because I was
the one
she wanted
all her life,
and
I was
not for her
and never
would be
just because
I could be...
all of her life.

Do women
puzzle you
as much as
they do me?

The Shortest Distance

A woman can't go in just
one direction at a time.

A woman can't travel
in a straight line.

A woman can be a butterfly
She can't be a train.

A woman can't love you
Without causing you pain.

Grown Ups

We are men and women now,
my friends and I. We are
astonished to find ourselves
in such a disgraceful state
as being fully grown and now
will be sneered at by kids
when we walk past them
in our grown up clothes
bulky suits and clunky shoes.
We will holler and fight
behind closed doors.
We will fart unapologetically
and pretend not to be drunk
when we stagger down the hall.

Who ever thought we would
end up this way, when we were
once heedless as puppies at play
or colts romping in a field?

Theology Of War

The killers are at it again,
dropping bombs,
shooting each other,
all to prove
who's God is greater.

What is it about God
that brings out
the worst in us?

I thought that was
supposed to be
the work of the devil.

This Holy Holiday Season

What is this time of year
when the nights are long
and the cold wind clear,
when we try so hard to be
the way we ought to be
every other time of the year?

What is this holiday spirit
but our yearning for the light
and the love that sustains us,
when things don't go right,
as we dreamed them yesterday,
and we fear what comes tomorrow.

It's not the gifts we exchange,
the cheerful greetings,
the feasts and parties.
It's the season when our hearts sing
the sacred songs of our soul,
in earnest honor of human love,
the only God
we do not have to imagine.

Today's Forecast

She dislikes
all kinds
of bad weather.

When it rains
she goes inside
out and when
the pain starts
she goes to pieces

Tremors

They are rapt in conversation,
possibly falling in love.
He says something funny
and she laughs aloud,
the melody of her voice enchanting
all of the others in the room.

Everyone turns to look at her.
She hates to be the center of attention.
It makes her nervous and
her lovely smile becomes a shield,
but her beauty won't protect her.
It only makes things worse.

Suddenly, she is disenchanted,
stone still like a deer about to bolt.
Her eyes sing in a cracked and
personal voice:
"I've never known anyone.
No one has ever known me."

Now he knows he is in love
and it is not going to be easy.

Try Harder

I shouldn't do this
he said
as he did
what he did.

This is wrong
he said
as he did it
anyway.

But it's fun
he said
as he did it
again.

Was it good
for you
too fast
or too slow?

It was okay
she said
one more time
I'll let you know.

He tried
and he tried
but this time
he couldn't.

She wasn't happy
about it,
but it wasn't
so bad.

She had fun
got what she
didn't even know
she wanted.

Don't tell him
but a man fails
at anything
a woman prevails.

Wounds Of War

I bear the marks and pain
of our brutal campaign,
of clashes and battles royal,
not Waterloo or Wounded Knee,
but conflagrations nonetheless.

I might still be riding high
If I had ducked that bullet,
deflected that blade.
How could one so lovely
leave such an ugly scar?

I won a battle or two
but lost the war
to a very friendly enemy.
You fooled me, fragged me,
really blew me up
like a roadside bomb.

I keep repeating
that weary old adage
whatever good it may do:
What does not kill me,
can break my heart in two.

Conscience

Of all the moments
of my imperfect life,
it's the embarrassments
I seem to remember most.
The shame of myriad things
large and small haunts me,
but why is a mere faux pas
equal to adultery,
a cold comment as bad as
breaking someone's heart?
Conscience, our evil twin,
supposed to make us better,
tortures me with glee.

Under Your Thumb

Now as I begin
to see clearly
How I don't exist
in your eyes
and probably
am somewhere near
the very edge
of your mind,
I think it time
we consider
getting me out
from under
your thumb.

You Don't Know You

Know yourself
people say
since Socrates
gave that advice
way back in the day.
But try as you might
with every method
and every device,
the last person
likely to know
who you are
almost certainly
is you.

So, ask anybody
who's known you
just who you are,
and they will get
closer than you
to what is true
about the real you,
because very few
can see what lies
behind their own eyes,
and that, baby,
is you.

But if you
really don't try,
don't think about it,
don't squint,
don't spy,
don't even care,

sooner or later
you may find
you do, by god,
know that guy.

Love Is Not

Love is not a river
not an ocean
not a body in the dark.

I will suspend this search
for a single incandescent soul
to light my way,
to warm myself by,

I will will go it alone.
I will live by the ocean.
I will work.
I will swim and ride.
I will drink myself happy
when I'm not,
and I will cry
if I have to,
but not for long.
Those days are gone.

And if by chance,
love or something like it
should suddenly appear,
I will view it
with a jaundiced eye.
I will stop
and frisk it,
like a cop searching
for a concealed gun.

Love is not
to be trusted
until proven innocent.

Unimaginable Magic

As a child in the country,
I would lie on my stomach
watching water bugs skate
on needle sharp legs
on a surfaceless stream.

I was too young to know
their enchanting performance
was a perfect demonstration
of some simple principal,
easily spoiled by explanation.

Now I lie on my bed,
with my wife and my child,
watching graceless men
lumber across the dusty
surface of the moon.

Their remarkable accomplishment
is based on science, certainly,
but when my wife asks the meaning
of some technical term
I don't answer her question.

I insist such impossible things
always will be magic to me.

We Fight

We fight
and
she handles me
easily,
as a quick mind
has a slight thought.

It rankles
to be so
overmatched,
but I 'm scrappy,
so I stay with her.

Generally,
I like her ways.

Finished

How can such simple things
end so painfully?
Friendships that turn
to real disaster.
Friends wanting only
what they need become monsters.

Afternoons that begin brightly
end in total dark.
Whole lives and fragments of lives
bracketed with tears.

I don't want to touch anything now
that has people in it.
Not a bed for making love
or one for dying.
Don't want to hear a song where
someone is mentioned fondly.

I want none of it! All bets are off!
I'll take less animate objects
like stones, trees, countrysides,
highways, ants, rainstorms...
things that end without crying out
or calling attention to themselves.

I Think I'll Go Now

I think I'll go now,
and take my memories with me.
My friends are all gone
There's no one here to miss me.

It's been lovely.
It's been a lot of fun.
It's been sometimes spectacular
but now I've got to run.

I paid my dues
I took my chances
sang my songs
and did my dances

I'm not proud of everything
but I'm also not ashamed.
I had my wild ways
but now they're mostly tamed.

I had my turns at love
and sometime love had me.
Nothing lasts forever
and all is vanity.

I think I'll go now
and take my memories with me.
All the girls I've known here,
now not a one to kiss me.

Goddess Of Love
to Jeanne

It may sound
like a fanciful movie
but you did appear
to me in a dream.

As I battled
my surrealist demons
you were above it all
smiling ambiguously
on the tumult
of my life.

You were silent
but your eyes
were radiant,
your arms open
as if to say:
I'll be here
when you are finished
fucking around.

We were longtime friends,
the one we trusted,
the one who
never questioned,
the one to turn to
when others
let us down.

I was not blameless
in my treatment
of other women,
but this is
about you and me.

The constant bond
as marriages ended,
affairs failed,
we would console
each other,
have a drink,
a smoke,
a meal
and try to laugh
it all away
or weep if it
was unavoidable.

We made love once.
It was good
and natural as
wind and fire,
but I was
or we were
not ready
so the spirit left
and it was years
before it came back.

I had always thought
lasting love impossible,
that passion withered,
then love died.

It took years
to realize
that being in love
with the goddess of love
could not possibly
end that way,
love.